CW01501737

The Lice Outbreak

The Avery Diary Book 2

By
Lucky Fish Press
Copyright ©2025

CONTENTS

1.The Announcement

It was just another typical Tuesday in the cafeteria—until it wasn't. The usual sounds of clinking trays, crinkling chip bags, and kids arguing over who stole the last chocolate pudding filled the air. I was busy inspecting a slightly suspicious glob of macaroni on my lunch tray when the loudspeaker crackled to life. Everyone froze. The entire school knew that Principal Walder never used the PA system unless it was either serious or seriously boring. But that day, it was definitely the former.

"Attention, students. This is your principal speaking. We have...a situation."

I glanced up, noodles dangling from my fork. You could have heard a pin drop. I wasn't sure if he was about to tell us that the cafeteria ran out of dessert or that the school was on fire, but whatever it was, it sounded dramatic.

"We have a confirmed case of lice in the school," he continued, his voice all serious and extra deep. "I repeat: lice."

Now, if you've never witnessed a room of seventh graders reacting to lice, let me tell you, it was like an apocalypse. I'm talking about total and complete chaos. Forks clattered. Trays flipped. Screaming erupted from Table 7, which was quickly followed by a chain reaction of people scratching their heads as if they'd just rolled through a field of fleas.

My best friends, Claire and Ellie, exchanged a panicked glance.

"Oh. My. Gosh. Lice!" Claire whisper-shouted, her eyes wide with horror.

"They can't actually spread in a school, right?" Ellie said, scratching her own head almost on instinct.

I tried not to scratch, but the more I thought about lice, the itchier my scalp became. Was it the power of suggestion, or was there already a tiny bug army setting up camp on my head?

Across the cafeteria, Jim Morley—a kid known for doing exactly the wrong thing at exactly the wrong time—was now standing on his chair, yelling, "I

3

have to get out of here! I can feel them crawling!" He then proceeded to shake his head like a wet dog, which only caused people to back away from him like he was ground zero for some kind of lice invasion.

"EVERYONE REMAIN CALM," Principal Walder's voice boomed over the PA system. That, of course, only made things worse. Tables were now splitting into smaller and smaller circles of kids who were checking each other's hair, accusing each other of "probably having it" and declaring their immunity in loud, triumphant voices.

Then there was Mackenzie Harper. She, of course, saw the entire situation as an opportunity to flaunt her "superiority," or whatever. Mackenzie was already standing on her lunch table, flipping her perfect, glossy hair and announcing, "Lice would never want my hair. Only gross people get lice!"

She looked right at me as she said it. Typical Mackenzie.

Claire nudged me, raising an eyebrow. "Only Mackenzie would make lice into some kind of status symbol."

I shrugged, scratching my head a little more. "Yeah, well, even lice have to have standards."

Around us, kids were pulling out their phones, Googling things like, "Can lice make you go bald?" and "Do lice like straight hair more than curly hair?" and "Does burning your hair keep lice away?" Just seeing the search results had me freaking out a little. Did lice actually lay hundreds of eggs? Did they really jump from person to person in a single bound?

The lunch aides tried to get things under control, but they were no match for the Great Lice Panic of Seventh Grade. One of the lunch ladies actually started scratching her own head, which only made things worse.

"I heard they can live on your head for like, YEARS," a kid at the next table whispered to his friend.

Ellie's eyes went huge. "Years? No way, I cannot have roommates living on my head for that long. I have enough trouble sharing my room with my sister!"

"Quiet down, everyone!" Principal Walder's voice boomed again, but the scratching frenzy had officially begun. Everyone around me was itching, clawing at their scalps like a group of cats that had just gotten wet.

In the middle of all this, I caught Mackenzie casting a disgusted look at her "inner circle"—a group of girls who followed her around like she was queen of the school. Mackenzie was still going on about how only "gross people" got lice, acting as if her perfectly styled hair was somehow above a parasitic insect.

Claire leaned over and whispered, "Bet you five dollars Mackenzie wouldn't even admit it if she did have lice."

"Please, she'd sooner shave her head than admit that," I said, rolling my eyes.

Meanwhile, my mind started wandering to horror scenarios of being dragged into the nurse's office and having my head searched by Mrs. Daniels, the school nurse, who wielded a flashlight and a lice comb like they were weapons of mass destruction. If Mrs. Barnaby found even one microscopic flake of dandruff, you were marked for life.

Suddenly, I felt a tug on my sleeve. It was Ellie, looking absolutely terrified.

"Avery, do you think I have it?" she whispered, her voice barely above a squeak. "I mean, I was scratching earlier...what if I'm the one who started it?"

I laughed nervously, trying to comfort her, but deep down, I was just as terrified. I leaned in and whispered, "Look, as long as we all stick together, we'll be fine. Plus, it's Mackenzie we should be worried about, not us."

Just then, Jim Morley sprinted by, screaming, "Lice! They're coming for us all!" as he slapped his own head like he was playing whack-a-mole. This was followed by more scratching, screaming, and chaos as kids tried to escape the imaginary lice that Jim had now convinced them were flying through the air like invisible drones.

That's when Principal Walder tried one last time. "Everyone, listen closely. We will have a mandatory lice inspection today in the nurse's office. Please remain calm and return to your classes."

Yeah, right. Remaining calm was officially impossible. Lice had somehow turned our school into a ticking time bomb of paranoia, complete with scratching, screaming, and the haunting image of Nurse Daniels' comb waiting for us all. I was already planning out excuses to skip the inspection.

But, as I found out later, lice would bring out a whole new level of drama, secrets, and, yep, itching. And somehow, I had a feeling this was only the beginning.

2.The Lice-Free Theory

Once the lice panic started, there was only one person who could make it worse: Mackenzie Harper. If there's one thing Mackenzie loves more than drama, it's drama she can use to make herself look like the queen of the school.

So there we were, scratching and freaking out, when Mackenzie stood up on her chair like it was her personal throne, clearing her throat in that loud, "I need everyone's attention" kind of way. She flicked her hair over her shoulder and started talking about the "scientific" reason why lice would never want her hair.

"Look, everyone," she announced, just loud enough for the cafeteria to go quiet, "lice don't just pick anyone. They only go for... uncool people." She paused for effect, making sure we all had time to process the idea that our level of "coolness" might determine our lice-attraction status. Then, just as a bunch of kids started scratching harder, she added, "So, yeah, I guess some of you might be... more at risk than others."

Claire turned to me, her mouth open. "Did Mackenzie just say lice have, like, standards?"

"Yes," I whispered back, trying not to laugh. "Apparently, lice only go for 'low quality hair' or something."

Mackenzie tossed her hair again, looking smug, and continued her speech. "I read about it in, like, a magazine. It's all about who's... you know... *Cooler*. Like, certain hair types are just not attractive to lice." She pointed to her own head as if we needed proof of her supposed "lice-repelling" hair.

The thing about Mackenzie is that once she gets an audience, there's no stopping her. It's like she goes into "Mackenzie Mode" where she thinks she's a celebrity being interviewed for Lice Weekly or something.

"Take my hair, for example," she continued, running her fingers through it with a look of pure admiration. "It's just... not the kind of hair lice would even consider living in. I mean, they'd be lucky, sure, but my hair is way too... classy."

"Classy hair?" I muttered to Ellie, who was trying to stifle her laughter.

"Next she'll say she's immune to mosquitoes," Ellie whispered back.

Meanwhile, other kids were starting to panic even more. People kept sneaking glances at Mackenzie, comparing their hair to hers and scratching furiously, as if the mere fact of not having Mackenzie's hair meant they were suddenly covered in bugs.

"I don't know, maybe she's right," said Mike Diaz, a kid who sits behind me in math class. "I mean, my cousin got lice, and he's definitely not what I'd call… 'cool.'" Mike was already scratching his head and looking around nervously, like he'd just discovered he was ground zero for uncool lice.

This was Mackenzie's cue to dial things up. She started walking around like some kind of lice-free goddess, inspecting the rest of us with what I can only describe as pity.

"Sorry, but… not everyone's hair is created equal," she said, looking at a girl from band who was scratching her head like a maniac. "Some people are just naturally more… susceptible."

Claire rolled her eyes so hard I thought they might get stuck. "Mackenzie's acting like she's got magic hair or something."

"Yeah," I whispered back. "Like lice look at her and go, 'Oh no, she's way too fabulous for us!'"

But Mackenzie wasn't done. "I mean, it's not like I'm saying anyone here definitely has lice," she continued, trying to sound sympathetic. "It's just, you know, certain types of people might want to, like, check."

By now, she was staring right at me, Ellie, and Claire. Because, of course, we're apparently the kind of "types" Mackenzie thinks lice would target.

"What's her deal?" Ellie whispered, scratching her head for the millionth time.

"I think she's trying to make lice a popularity contest," I replied.

Mackenzie just kept going. "Lice are drawn to certain behaviors, too," she added, giving a dramatic sigh. "Like, you know, people who don't wash their hair enough, or people who... well, don't have the kind of hair that lice respect."

"Respect?" Claire choked, barely able to contain her laughter. "Is she serious right now?"

"Oh, she's serious," I said, watching as Mackenzie's friends, the "Mackenzie Minions" as we call them, gathered around her, nodding like she was delivering some kind of revolutionary lice theory.

It wasn't long before Mackenzie's theory spread faster than... well, lice. Kids all over the cafeteria were now looking at each other suspiciously, judging each other's "coolness" based on scratch frequency. And Mackenzie was just eating it up.

"Oh, Avery, you're scratching a lot," she said with a smile that was all teeth and no sympathy. "You know, they say scratching is the first sign."

I shot back, "Or maybe it's just because I'm listening to you talk about lice nonstop."

Ellie giggled, but Mackenzie didn't look too pleased. "I'm just saying, Avery," she said, loud enough for everyone to hear. "If you start seeing little white dots in your hair... maybe consider what type of people lice are attracted to."

I wanted to launch a comeback, but just then, the lunch aide started coming around, reminding everyone to calm down and stop scratching.

"This is turning into a nightmare," Claire whispered. "At this rate, everyone in school is going to think they have lice."

"Oh, they definitely will," I replied, rolling my eyes. "Thanks to Mackenzie's 'cool people don't get lice' theory, which, by the way, might be the dumbest thing I've ever heard."

Just then, Mackenzie's friend Julia spoke up, "Mackenzie, you're so right. Lice are totally not into people with, like, awesome hair. I heard they hate the smell of conditioner."

"Oh, I read that, too," Mackenzie said, nodding like she'd just heard the most brilliant idea. "That's why I condition every day."

The whole cafeteria was now buzzing with lice-related rumors. Kids were trading tips about which shampoos were "lice-repellent," debating whether hats would "trap lice," and discussing their theories on what kinds of hairstyles might make them safe.

Meanwhile, Mackenzie continued her "lice don't like me" routine, swishing her hair and giving people sympathetic smiles that were, honestly, just annoying.

"Lice are just, like… particular," she concluded, sounding like she'd just delivered the wisdom of the ages. "Some of us have resistant hair, and some… well, some don't." She gave one final, pitying look at our table and then pranced off, her minions trailing behind her.

As she walked away, I turned to Ellie and said, "You know, maybe lice do have standards."

Ellie raised an eyebrow. "What do you mean?"

"Well, they're smart enough to stay away from Mackenzie."

Ellie and Claire burst out laughing, and we all scratched our heads, trying to ignore the fact that Mackenzie's speech had somehow made us itch even more.

And thanks to her, I realized that surviving this lice outbreak was going to be just as much about dodging her "cool person" speeches as it was about avoiding the actual bugs.

3. The Lice Detective

By the time I got home, I was done. Between Principal Walder's lice panic speech, Mackenzie's "cool people don't get lice" theory, and my head feeling like it was itching on command, all I wanted was a lice-free zone to chill out in. Unfortunately, the one person who could ruin my plans was sitting on the living room floor, surrounded by Legos: my little brother Carl.

I barely got two steps into the house before Carl spotted me. "Hey, Avery!" he called, running over, his feet somehow missing every single Lego piece like some kinda annoying ninja.

Mom barely looked up, just nodded. "Oh no, lice? That's never fun. Make sure you don't share hats with anyone."

Hats? Who did she think I was, some kind of rookie? "Mom, it's worse than that," I said, grabbing an apple from the grocery bag. "We're talking mass hysteria. Mackenzie Harper even invented this whole 'cool people don't get lice' theory and practically crowned herself the Lice Queen."

Mom laughed a little, but before she could respond, Carl zoomed in, apparently listening in on our *private* conversation like it was his job.

"LICE?" Carl gasped, his eyes wide like he'd just won the lottery. "That's AMAZING!"

"Um, no, Carl, lice are *not* amazing," I said, already regretting saying anything within his hearing range.

Carl ignored me, his face lighting up with a wicked grin. "Avery, this is it! I'm going to catch the Lice Monsters!"

Before I could stop him, Carl dashed out of the kitchen like a man on a mission. I could only imagine what he had in mind, and knowing Carl, it wouldn't be good. I turned back to Mom, rolling my eyes. "Carl's being Carl again."

Not even two minutes later, Carl reappeared, proudly wearing a *colander* on his head. He had his little toy flashlight in one hand and his magnifying glass in the other, like he was ready to solve the Mystery of the Lice.

"Carl," I groaned, "why do you have a *colander* on your head?"

"Protection," he declared. "The Lice Monsters can't get through the holes! It's like a lice force field."

I smacked my forehead. "Carl, that's...not how lice work."

But he was already in "Lice Detective" mode. "Avery," he said, his voice all serious, "hold still. I need to inspect your head. Just to be sure."

"Carl, you don't even know what you're looking for."

"Of course I do! I've seen bugs. They have legs and creepy little eyes. Lice are basically tiny aliens!"

"Yeah, Carl. Totally. Tiny aliens who travel *exclusively* by hair," I muttered.

"Exactly!" Carl shouted, taking this as total confirmation of his theory. He shoved his flashlight about two inches from my eyeball, temporarily blinding me. "Hold still, this is a very *technical* inspection."

"Carl, get that flashlight out of my face!" I yelped, swatting his hand away.

He squinted through the magnifying glass, pressing his nose so close to my scalp that I was pretty sure he was actually going to sniff my hair. "Hmm. I don't see any yet, but that's exactly what a Lice Monster *wants* you to think."

This time, I rolled my eyes so hard I practically saw my brain. "Carl, there are no 'Lice Monsters.' You're just making things up."

He ignored me and tapped his flashlight against my head as if testing my skull for *lice sounds.* "No, no, I'm onto something big here," he said, grinning. "You see, lice are sneaky. They hide until they think it's safe to come out. But not today. Not on my watch."

"Carl, that doesn't even make sense."

"Shhh! I think I heard one move," he whispered, pressing his ear to my head as if a lice was going to say, "Hello, Carl!" and introduce itself. "They're probably forming a plan right now."

By this point, Mom was watching us from the counter, trying not to laugh. "Looks like you've got a very determined Lice Detective there, Avery."

I groaned. "Mom, please tell him to knock it off."

But she just shrugged. "Carl, leave your sister alone."

Carl didn't even bother defending himself. He was too busy running his magnifying glass over my head, giving me updates on his "lice investigation."

"Avery, don't move. I need to scan for lice fingerprints," he said, frowning in concentration.

"Lice don't have *fingers,* Carl."

"You don't know that!" he replied. "Maybe they're *microscopic* fingers. That's why they're so good at sneaking around."

This was starting to get out of hand. "Carl, I'm pretty sure your 'lice fingerprint' theory isn't...scientifically accurate."

He ignored me, reaching into his pocket to pull out what looked like a tiny notebook. "Day one of the Lice Monster Investigation," he muttered, scribbling furiously. "Subject: Avery. Head Status: Itchy. Possible signs of tiny alien invasion. Further investigation needed."

"Carl, are you writing a *lice diary* about me?" I asked, horrified.

Carl shrugged. "Someone's gotta keep track, Avery. Today it's you, tomorrow it could be Mom. Or Dad. Or *even me.*" He shivered dramatically, like the very thought of lice on his head was too much to bear.

"Maybe you should inspect *your* head next, Detective Carl," I suggested, hoping he'd drop the investigation on me.

He backed up, looking horrified. "No way! If I have lice, they'll know I'm onto them! They might do something drastic!"

"Yeah, like what? Host a mini parade across your scalp?"

Carl gasped. "Exactly. And I don't want to give them the satisfaction."

Finally, he stepped back, tilting his colander helmet to a more "serious" angle. "All right, Avery, you're in the clear... *for now.* But I'll be keeping my eyes on you. Remember: lice never sleep."

"Good to know, Carl," I said, trying not to laugh.

As he left the room, he turned back one last time, raising his flashlight dramatically. "And remember, if you feel something crawling... it might just be the *Lice Monsters.*"

Once he was finally gone, I sighed in relief. Only in my house could a lice panic turn into a full-scale "Lice Monster Investigation" with my little brother as the lead detective.

Mom just shook her head, laughing. "At least he's keeping you entertained."

"Yeah, but if he calls me 'Subject Avery' one more time, I'm shaving his head in his sleep."

As I walked away, I caught Carl in the hall, already practicing his "lice search" techniques on his stuffed animals. And even though he was the most annoying brother ever, I had to admit, Detective Carl was definitely one of a kind.

4. The Great Lice Inspection Showdown

The moment we walked into the nurse's office, I knew this wasn't going to be an ordinary checkup. There she was, Nurse Daniels, our school's "health enforcer," ready with her *giant flashlight,* her oversized tweezers, and—get this—her very own "lice inspection" headband with a single wobbly magnifying glass sticking up in front. The whole setup made her look like a crazy scientist about to perform some kind of bug surgery.

Our entire class was lined up against the wall. The room was so quiet you could hear the sound of a hundred nervous fingers scratching behind ears, on necks, and under collars. Every kid in line was either staring straight ahead or looking down.

"Alright, kids!" Nurse Daniels barked, looking a little too excited. "Today, we're going to make sure no lice have set up camp in this school. When I call your name, step forward, and don't even *think* about scratching!"

I froze, willing myself to keep my hands at my sides. It was like when someone says, "Don't think about pink elephants," and suddenly, all you can see are pink elephants. All I could think about was *how itchy* I was. I shot Ellie a desperate look, hoping she'd have some magic trick for not scratching, but she was already digging into her scalp with both hands. Great start.

Then, a little voice from the back of the line squeaked, "Carl says if you wear a pot on your head, the lice can't get to your brain."

I turned around and, sure enough, a bunch of kids had taken Carl's "lice shield" idea way too seriously. A kid named Tommy had on a mixing bowl, another was wearing a spaghetti strainer, and one poor girl was hiding under an empty popcorn bag. It was like a parade of mini Carl clones, each with their very own kitchenware helmet.

Nurse Daniels noticed too, and her eyes narrowed. "Take those *hats* off right now!" she yelled, but they just clutched their armor tighter.

"I'm not letting the lice steal my thoughts!" Tommy yelled back, and a few other kids started nodding along, looking ready to defend themselves to the death if necessary.

The whole line was itching to get out of there—literally—and that only seemed to add fuel to the fire. "Alright, Anderson, step forward!" Nurse Daniels commanded, and the poor kid practically stumbled up, scratching behind his ear like his life depended on it.

Nurse Daniels tilted his head and started going through his hair like she was searching for gold. Every so often, she'd let out a "hmmm" or a "tsk tsk," and Anderson looked like he was about to pass out. Finally, she stepped back, squinted, and nodded, clearly disappointed. "Lice-free!" she announced, sounding almost a little sad about it.

I sighed in relief. So far, so good. But just as I was starting to relax, I noticed Ellie next to me scratching her head like she was trying to dig her way out of a prison cell.

"Ellie, *stop scratching*," I whispered, nudging her. "You're going to look like Patient Zero!"

But Ellie's scratching just got worse. "I can't help it, Avery! My head feels like it's on fire!"

I tried to think of a distraction. "Pretend you're, like, the coolest person ever. Cool people don't scratch, right? Look at Mackenzie Harper; she practically *sashayed* through the cafeteria, acting like she was too good for lice."

Ellie took a deep breath, nodding. "Right, right. I'm cool. Cool people don't scratch." She closed her eyes, took a calming breath, and... immediately started scratching again, even harder this time.

It was no use. As soon as Nurse Daniels called Ellie's name, she practically tripped over her own feet, scratching her head so wildly that Nurse Daniels just shook her head, muttering something about "itchy kids." With a flashlight in one hand and her oversized tweezers in the other, Nurse Daniels went to work, diving into Ellie's hair with an intensity that made even *me* nervous.

Ellie, looking panicked, turned and whispered to me, "If I have lice, promise you won't tell anyone?"

"Cross my heart," I whispered back, but deep down, I knew that if Ellie ended up with lice, the entire school would know by lunchtime. It was like the worst secret you could ever try to keep.

Finally, it was my turn. I took a deep breath and stepped forward, trying to act as nonchalant as possible. "Just another day at school," I told myself, even though I could feel the other kids staring at me like I was about to go on trial.

Nurse Daniels looked me over, flashlight at the ready, and got to work. She leaned in so close, squinting at my scalp like she was looking for hidden treasure.

"What's this?" she said, pulling back and holding up her flashlight with the kind of intensity that made my heart stop.

I froze. "What? What's what?"

Nurse Daniels took a closer look, her expression a mix of surprise and suspicion. "Is this... glitter?"

I gulped. Right. I'd completely forgotten that last weekend I'd done that glitter art project, and, well, let's just say I hadn't quite managed to get rid of every last sparkle.

"Yes, um, glitter. I'm really into, uh, sparkle art?"

Nurse Daniels raised an eyebrow but finally gave up. "Well, it's *not* lice," she said, sounding disappointed, and moved on. I let out a sigh of relief, but my relief didn't last long.

Just as Nurse Daniels declared me officially lice-free, a kid in the back shrieked, 'I see one crawling!' and all chaos erupted like someone had just yelled 'FIRE!' in a movie theater.

Kids started screaming, jumping out of line, scratching like they were in the middle of a full-blown lice zombie apocalypse. Nurse Daniels tried to calm everyone down, waving her flashlight and shouting, "It's just lavender spray! Stay in line!"

But it was no use. Half the class had already bolted, running for the door, convinced that lice were about to launch a full-scale attack.

The poor first graders in their makeshift helmets were the only ones who stayed put, each clutching their colanders and bowls like brave little warriors. One of them yelled, "See? We're safe!" while everyone else ran around scratching like they'd never scratched before.

I made my escape in the chaos, managing to slip past Nurse Daniels and her "lice-taming" lavender spray. But as I left the nurse's office, I couldn't shake the feeling that this lice inspection madness was far from over.

5. The Crown Slips

Gym class is usually one of my least favorite parts of the day. Between dodgeballs flying at your head and the sweaty smell that somehow lingers even after everyone's gone, it's basically a torture chamber with squeaky sneakers. But today, something way more interesting caught my attention.

It started during warm-ups when I spotted Mackenzie Harper—yes, THE Mackenzie Harper—looking suspiciously twitchy. Now, Mackenzie never looks anything less than perfect, even during gym class. Her hair is always shiny, her outfit always coordinated, and her confidence dialed up to a hundred. She's the kind of person who probably wakes up with perfect eyeliner and fresh lip gloss. But today? Oh no. Today was different.

Mackenzie was scratching. And not just a little scratch here or there—she was scratching like her life depended on it. She'd go in for a quick head-scratch and then stop, glancing around like she thought someone might be watching. Spoiler alert: *I was definitely watching.*

"Ellie, Claire," I hissed, nudging them during stretches. "Is it just me, or is Mackenzie...itchy?"

Ellie peeked over at Mackenzie and nearly fell out of her stretch. "Whoa, you're right," she whispered back. "That's not a normal amount of scratching."

Claire squinted, trying to get a better look. "Do you think she...?"

"Has lice?" I finished, my voice dropping to a dramatic whisper. "Oh, I *definitely* think she does."

We all stared, trying to be subtle but failing miserably. Mackenzie must have felt our eyes on her because she suddenly froze mid-scratch and tossed her hair over her shoulder in that dramatic way she always does, like she's in a shampoo commercial. Except today, her hair wasn't smooth and shiny—it was a tangled, frizzy mess.

"Whoa," Ellie said, eyes wide. "Is it just me, or does her hair look like it lost a fight with a leaf blower?"

"She probably blames the humidity," Claire whispered, but I could tell she was just as shocked as we were.

For the rest of gym class, Mackenzie kept scratching, but she was trying *way* too hard to act like she wasn't. She even faked a yawn at one point and used it as an excuse to casually rake her nails through her scalp. Nice try, Mackenzie. We weren't buying it.

After gym, we headed to the locker room, and that's when things got even weirder. Mackenzie pulled a baseball cap out of her bag and shoved it on her head like she was trying to hide something. Now, I don't know if you've ever seen Mackenzie Harper wear a baseball cap, but let me tell you—it was *not* her style. This is the girl who once called a perfectly normal hoodie "too casual." So, yeah, a hat? That was suspicious.

"She's definitely hiding something," Ellie said as we watched Mackenzie adjust her cap in the mirror.

Claire nodded. "Do you think she's scared the lice are going to parachute out of her hair or something?"

I laughed, but honestly, the image of little lice with tiny parachutes was kind of stuck in my head after that.

After gym, we headed to the cafeteria for lunch. Normally, Mackenzie would sit at her usual table in the center of the room, surrounded by her loyal followers. But today? She plopped down at the far corner table, practically hiding behind her tray of organic kale salad.

"Okay, this is getting weirder by the minute," I said, grabbing my PB&J and apple. "She's avoiding people now. Mackenzie Harper doesn't *avoid* people. People avoid *her.*"

"Maybe she's just having an off day," Claire suggested.

"Yeah," Ellie added. "An off day... full of *scratching* and *hats* and *hiding.*"

We all turned to look at Mackenzie, who was poking at her salad like it had personally insulted her. She glanced around the room nervously before sneaking another scratch under the brim of her hat.

"Busted," I whispered, grinning.

As we ate, the pieces started coming together. The scratching, the messy hair, the hat—it all pointed to one thing. Queen bee Mackenzie Harper, had lice.

Later that afternoon, during math class, Mackenzie's scratching reached a whole new level. Mrs. Porter was in the middle of explaining something about fractions when Mackenzie suddenly ducked her head under her desk and scratched furiously.

I leaned over to Ellie and whispered, "She's gone full monkey mode."

Ellie snorted so loud that Mrs. Porter stopped mid-sentence and gave her one of those *teacher glares* that could melt steel.

"Something you'd like to share with the class, Ellie?"

"No, ma'am," Ellie mumbled, her face turning bright red.

Mackenzie, meanwhile, popped back up like nothing had happened, pretending to be super interested in her notebook. I almost felt bad for her. Almost.

By the end of the day, I was practically bursting to tell someone— anyone—about my discovery. But at the same time, I knew I couldn't. If Mackenzie really did have lice, the news would spread faster than, well, lice. And as much as I didn't like her, I couldn't imagine how embarrassing it would be for her if the whole school found out.

Still, I couldn't shake the feeling that this lice outbreak was about to get *a lot* more interesting.

6. Lice, Lies, and Lavender

If I thought Mackenzie was acting weird before, the next few days proved I hadn't seen anything yet. The moment she walked into class on Monday morning, it was like someone had turned her into a walking advertisement for "Lice Repellent Spray: Now With Extra Paranoia." She marched in, spritzing the air around her like she was warding off mosquitoes at a summer barbecue.

"Everyone, stand back!" she announced, waving the spray can dramatically. "This is for your own safety. I'm creating a *lice-free zone.*"

The entire class stared as Mackenzie sprayed her hair, her desk, and even the pencil sharpener. I'm pretty sure the only thing she didn't spray was the class hamster, Mr. Paws, but that was probably because he was in his cage.

Of course, her loyal followers, Bella and Sasha, were all over it.

"Oh my gosh, Mackenzie, you're so smart," Bella said, holding her nose as the overwhelming scent of lavender filled the room. "I didn't even know lice hated lavender!"

"They probably hate it because it's so... exclusive," Sasha added, flipping her hair like that made sense.

Meanwhile, the rest of us were coughing like we'd wandered into a perfume factory explosion.

"Is this supposed to repel lice or just choke them out?" I whispered to Ellie, who was fanning herself with a math book.

By lunchtime, things had gotten even more ridiculous. Mackenzie had set up a "lice-free table" in the cafeteria, complete with a handmade glittery sign that read *NO ITCHIES ALLOWED.* She made Bella and Sasha stand guard while she adjusted her latest hat—a sparkly pink beret that looked like it belonged to a French poodle.

"Only cool kids who *definitely* don't have lice can sit here," Mackenzie declared, spraying her sandwich with the repellent for good measure.

I couldn't help but laugh. "Did she just spray her turkey wrap?" I asked Claire, who was already trying to sneak a picture on her phone.

"Maybe she's worried the lice are branching out into poultry," Claire joked.

Ellie leaned over. "You know what's weird? She didn't even start this whole lice paranoia thing until *after* the nurse checks. Like, she was totally chill before then."

That's when it hit me. Mackenzie wasn't trying to prevent lice—she was trying to *cover them up.*

The next day, Mackenzie rolled into school wearing the biggest hat I'd ever seen. It was a rhinestone-covered cowboy hat, complete with fringe, and it looked like something you'd see at a glitter rodeo. She even tilted it forward dramatically, like she was in some kind of undercover spy movie.

"Is she trying to hide lice or smuggle a watermelon under there?" Claire whispered as we watched her strut into homeroom.

Mackenzie didn't stop at the hat, either. She'd added sunglasses and a scarf, making her look like she was on the run from the paparazzi. "Ugh, it's just so hard being a trendsetter," she sighed loudly, adjusting her hat for the hundredth time.

"You think she's hiding lice under all that, don't you?" Ellie asked me.

"I don't *think* she is," I said. "I *know* she is."

Later, during science class, things got even weirder. We were supposed to be working on a group project about ecosystems, but Mackenzie spent the entire time scratching her head and accusing random things of being lice carriers.

"Did you know lice can travel on pets?" she asked dramatically, pointing at the hamster cage. "Mr. Paws is probably the real source of this outbreak!"

Poor Mr. Paws froze mid-wheel run, his little hamster eyes wide with fear.

"Leave the hamster alone, Mackenzie," our teacher, Mrs. Sawyer, said with a sigh. "He doesn't even have hair long enough for lice to survive on."

"That's exactly what the lice *want* you to think," Mackenzie replied, narrowing her eyes at the cage.

At this point, Bella and Sasha were nodding along like Mackenzie was some kind of lice conspiracy expert. Meanwhile, I was struggling to keep a straight face.

But the real cherry on the "Mackenzie has lice" sundae came during art class. We were supposed to be painting self-portraits, but Mackenzie had other plans.

Instead of painting herself, she painted...a bottle of lice spray.

"Is that...a still life of bug spray?" Ellie asked, leaning over to get a better look.

"It's symbolic," Mackenzie said, swirling her brush dramatically. "It represents my commitment to staying lice-free. Not everyone can relate."

I had to bite my lip to keep from laughing. If this wasn't proof that Mackenzie was hiding something, I didn't know what was.

By the end of the day, I was practically bursting to tell someone about my theory. But at the same time, I wasn't totally sure what to do with this information. If Mackenzie really did have lice, announcing it to the whole school would probably be the nuclear option. As much as I didn't like her, I couldn't imagine how humiliating that would be.

Still, one thing was clear: Mackenzie's days as the "cool, untouchable queen bee" were officially numbered. The itch investigation had begun, and I was determined to get to the bottom of it.

7. Secrets, Scratches, and Mayo Madness

If there's one thing middle school teaches you, it's that secrets are basically social dynamite. Mackenzie's itchy little secret could blow the roof off this school, and part of me really wanted to light that fuse.

I mean, let's be real—Mackenzie deserved it. She'd spent the past week acting like the President of the Lice-Free World, making snarky comments about "lice losers" and bragging about how "the cool crowd" was immune to infestations. And yet, here she was, scratching her head like it was a lottery ticket.

But then I thought about what would happen if I exposed her. Imagine having the entire school know you were crawling with lice. That's the kind of reputation-destroying scandal people would still be talking about at our high school reunion.

And honestly? If it were me, I'd probably move to another country and change my name to avoid the humiliation.

I was still debating what to do when I got home, only to find the situation at *my* house wasn't exactly a stress-free zone.

The second I walked into the kitchen, I heard Carl yelling, "PETE, GET THE MAYO!"

This is never a sentence you want to hear.

"What is going on?" I asked, dropping my backpack.

Carl was standing on a stool next to the counter, holding an industrial-sized jar of mayonnaise. His best friend Pete was sitting at the table, wearing a shower cap smeared with what I assumed was said mayo. Whiskers, our grumpy cat, was sprawled on the counter, licking at a blob of mayonnaise someone had apparently spilled.

"It's a lice treatment!" Carl announced, grinning like he'd just invented sliced bread. "Pete thinks he might have lice, so we're using mayo to smother them. I saw it on YouTube."

Pete waved at me, the shower cap slipping sideways. "Hey, Avery. I can already feel it working."

"That's the mayo, Pete," I said. "Not magic."

My mom walked in at that moment and nearly dropped the grocery bags she was holding.

"Carl! Why is Whiskers covered in mayonnaise?"

Carl looked offended. "He's not covered, Mom. It's just a little bit. Whiskers doesn't like lice either."

"Whiskers doesn't even *have* lice!" Mom exclaimed, trying to grab the cat, who immediately jumped onto the fridge to avoid her. Now the fridge door had a greasy paw print on it.

"Better safe than sorry," Carl said with a shrug.

Mom gave me a look that said, *Why is this my life?* I could only shrug back.

After dinner, Carl's mayo madness continued. He'd roped Pete into an experiment to see how long you could keep mayonnaise on your head before it dried out. The answer, according to Carl, was "as long as possible."

At one point, he came into the living room, holding a timer and wearing what looked like an entire roll of plastic wrap around his head.

"Do you think this will give me super lice powers?" he asked, striking a pose.

"Super powers like what? Attracting sandwiches?" I said, not even looking up from my homework.

Carl grinned. "No, like being able to spot lice from a mile away! Pete and I could start a business. *Lice Detectives: Solving Cases One Scratch at a Time.*"

Pete appeared behind him, nodding enthusiastically. "We'd make millions."

I groaned. "Please just go wash your hair before you clog the shower drain with mayonnaise."

Carl ran out of the room yelling, "That's why we have plungers!"

Even with all the chaos at home, my mind kept wandering back to Mackenzie. The next day at school, I saw her in the hallway, still rocking her over-the-top lice-defense accessories. Today's look? A floppy sunhat and matching scarf that made her look like she was about to star in a sunscreen commercial.

She caught me staring and flipped her hair dramatically. "Like my new hat, Avery? It's vintage."

"Uh-huh," I said, biting back a laugh.

The thing is, Mackenzie was so wrapped up in her own drama that she didn't even notice how obvious she was being. The scratching, the sudden obsession with hats, the gallons of lice spray—she might as well have been wearing a neon sign that said, *I HAVE LICE.*

At lunch, I sat with Claire and Ellie, still debating whether to spill the beans about Mackenzie.

"You're awfully quiet," Ellie said, poking her sandwich with a fork. "What's on your mind? Or should I say *who's* on your mind?"

I rolled my eyes. "It's not a *who.* It's a *what.* Specifically, lice."

Claire wrinkled her nose. "Ew. Please don't ruin lunch for me."

"I think Mackenzie has lice," I blurted.

Ellie raised an eyebrow. "You think? Or you *know*?"

"I mean, look at her," I said, gesturing across the cafeteria. Mackenzie was sitting at her glitter-covered "lice-free table," wearing yet another hat (this time a wide-brimmed fedora) and spraying her hair like she was putting out a fire.

Ellie and Claire turned to look, and Ellie burst out laughing. "Oh yeah, she's definitely got something going on. That's her *fifth* hat this week!"

Claire sighed. "So, what are you going to do about it?"

I shrugged. "Nothing. Yet."

Keeping quiet wasn't exactly easy, though, especially when Mackenzie kept doubling down on her "lice-free" act. During gym class, she refused to put her head on the wrestling mats, claiming they were "a breeding ground for lice." Then she started handing out "lice safety tips" during study hall, complete with homemade brochures that had glittery clip art and her signature at the bottom.

"She's handing these out like it's a campaign," I whispered to Claire as we watched Mackenzie work the room.

"Vote Mackenzie for Lice President," Claire joked.

By the time I got home that afternoon, I was exhausted. Carl and Pete, however, were still going strong with their "lice detective" antics. I found them in the bathroom, armed with magnifying glasses and wearing homemade badges that said *Official Lice Investigators*.

"What now?" I asked, leaning against the doorframe.

"We're testing out a new method," Carl said, pointing to a bowl of vinegar. "Apparently, lice hate vinegar. Pete's going to dip his hair in it."

Pete grinned. "This is gonna be epic."

I shook my head. "You guys are insane."

"Insanely brilliant," Carl corrected.

As much as I wanted to deny it, I couldn't help but laugh. If nothing else, this lice outbreak was turning into the weirdest, funniest circus I'd ever been stuck in.

8. Lice Awareness: The Musical (Sort Of)

By the time I got to school the next morning, I had a plan. Well, sort of. It wasn't the kind of plan you'd submit to NASA, but it was good enough for middle school.

I found Claire and Ellie by the lockers, and they were already scratching their heads (from nerves, not lice—I think).

"Okay, guys," I said, slamming my locker shut. "I've got an idea. What if we turned this whole lice mess into something fun?"

Ellie blinked. "Lice. Fun. Those words don't belong in the same sentence."

"Just hear me out," I said, waving my hands like some kind of motivational speaker. "We do an *Anti-Itch Week.* Hat days, scarf days, maybe even a dance! It'll take the focus off who might have lice and put it on, like, celebrating...not itching?"

Claire tilted her head. "You had me until 'celebrating not itching.' But go on."

"We can make it silly," I said, warming up to my own idea. "Posters, events, even a guest speaker. Maybe one of the teachers could share their 'lice survivor' story from back in the day. You know, to inspire us."

Ellie's eyes lit up. "Like an *Itchy Ted Talk*!"

We got to work immediately. By "we," I mean mostly Ellie, who is a poster-making wizard, and Claire, who's weirdly good at coming up with catchy slogans.

Our first stop was the art room, where we raided the supply closet for markers, glitter, and a roll of butcher paper big enough to wallpaper a house. Ellie sprawled on the floor, sketching out a cartoon lice with a big "X" over it. Underneath, she wrote: *Anti-Itch Week: Hats On, Scratch Off!*

Claire, meanwhile, was brainstorming event ideas. "What about a 'Lice-Free Lunchtime?' Everyone wears hats and eats outdoors so we don't, like, contaminate the cafeteria."

Ellie frowned. "That's just lunch, Claire."

"Fine, what about a contest?" Claire said. "Best Hat gets a prize. Like, I don't know, free pudding cups for a week."

"Sold," I said. "Who doesn't love pudding?"

We were so busy planning that I didn't even notice the time until the bell rang. As I ran to class, clutching a glittery poster that said *Dance the Itch Away!*, I bumped into Mr. Jenson, the history teacher.

"What's this, Miss Avery?" he asked, peering at the poster like it was written in hieroglyphics.

"We're organizing Anti-Itch Week!" I said. "To, uh, bring the school together."

He scratched his chin thoughtfully. "You know, I had lice when I was in sixth grade. Worst three months of my life."

"Three months?!" I squeaked.

"Back in my day, we didn't have these fancy sprays and shampoos," he said. "My mom used kerosene and a fine-toothed comb. Nearly set my head on fire!"

I nodded politely, backing away slowly. "That's...uh...inspiring. Thanks, Mr. Jenson!"

By lunchtime, news of Anti-Itch Week had spread faster than gossip about who failed math class. People were already brainstorming their hat ideas, and the cafeteria was buzzing with excitement. Even Mackenzie looked intrigued, though she was still wearing her signature sunhat and spraying her hair with enough "lice repellent" to make the air smell like a lavender explosion.

Claire and Ellie joined me at our table, where I was finishing up another poster.

"Okay," I said, holding it up. "What do you think of this one? *Lice Can't Dance, But We Can!*"

Ellie snorted. "This is so silly. I love it."

When I got home that afternoon, I was greeted by chaos. Again.

Carl and Pete were in the bathroom, and it looked like a food bomb had gone off.

"What now?" I asked, staring at the mess.

"We're perfecting the mayo mask," Carl said, gesturing to his head, which was wrapped in tin foil like he was auditioning for a sci-fi movie.

Pete was holding a bottle of mustard. "We're adding mustard this time. For extra power."

"That's not how science works," I said, grabbing a towel to clean up the mess.

Whiskers, who had somehow gotten mustard on his tail, screamed and bolted into the living room. My mom walked in just in time to see him streak past.

"Carl!" she shouted. "Why does the cat smell like a hot dog?!"

Carl shrugged. "He wanted to be part of the experiment."

"Whiskers did not sign up for this," I muttered, scrubbing mustard off the sink.

Despite the madness at home, Anti-Itch Week was shaping up to be a success. By Friday, the posters were up, the dance was scheduled, and Mr. Jenson had even agreed to be our guest speaker.

"I'll bring my kerosene story," he said, winking.

"Please don't," I replied.

The best part? People were actually excited. For the first time all week, it felt like the lice drama wasn't completely taking over.

At lunch, I noticed Mackenzie sitting with her friends, looking quieter than usual. She kept adjusting her hat and fiddling with her hair, which was definitely not her normal "queen bee" vibe.

Ellie leaned over and whispered, "Do you think she'll show up to the dance?"

"Maybe," I said, watching as Mackenzie tugged her hat a little lower. "But if she does, she better bring her best hat game. This school is ready to get creative!"

Claire grinned. "I mean, who wouldn't want to win Best Hat? Even Mackenzie probably has something fabulous up her sleeve."

We all chuckled, the kind of laugh that felt like we were finally lightening up about the whole lice madness. For the first time in days, it felt like we were all on the same team—just trying to get through the itch-pocalypse together.

9. The Epic Lice Brainstorm (and Cat Chaos)

Saturday afternoon at my house started out normal enough. Claire and Ellie came over to help finalize plans for Anti-Itch Week, but "normal" went out the window the second Carl and Pete showed up with a giant jar of... mayonnaise.

"Good news!" Carl announced, slamming the jar on the kitchen counter. "Pete and I have discovered the ultimate lice cure: mayo hair masks!"

"Bad news," Pete added. "We didn't think to check if Whiskers likes mayonnaise."

Right on cue, Whiskers launched himself at the bag like a furry missile. The next thirty seconds were a blur of paws, claws, and slippery mayo packets flying everywhere.

"Whiskers, NO!" I yelled, trying to grab him, but he leapt onto the fridge with a packet hanging from his mouth like a trophy. Pete saluted him. "The first casualty of the Anti-Itch War."

Ellie, meanwhile, had taken out her sketchpad. "Mayo-inspired hats," she muttered, furiously sketching. "A chef's hat... ooh, or one shaped like a mayonnaise jar!"

"Ellie," Claire said, deadpan, "if you wear a jar on your head, I'm pretending I don't know you."

Before we could argue, Carl dragged us all into the living room. He'd turned it into his "lice research lab," complete with posters of bug anatomy and a giant model of a lice comb made out of popsicle sticks.

"Welcome to the Lice Busters Headquarters!" Carl declared, handing out badges made of paper plates. Mine said *Chief Complainer*.

"Why am I the Chief Complainer?" I asked.

"Because you never stop whining about me," Carl said with a grin.

Pete was already setting up his boombox in the corner. "While the Chief Complainer does her thing, I've got something to lighten the mood. Behold—*DJ Scratch* presents: The Lice Rap!"

He hit play, and a beat that sounded suspiciously like "Ice Ice Baby" blasted through the room. Pete grabbed a spatula like a microphone and started rapping.

♪ "Yo, lice in your hair,
don't despair, just prepare,
Slap on some mayo, and show you care!" ♪

Claire and Ellie were doubled over laughing, and even I couldn't help cracking a smile. Carl, of course, thought it was the greatest thing ever and started beatboxing terribly. Whiskers, still holding his mayo packet, swished his tail in disapproval.

"Pete," I said, "I'm begging you—never do that in public."

"Too late," Pete said, grinning. "I'm performing it at the Anti-Itch Dance."

Claire groaned. "Avery, you have to stop him."

"No way," I said. "I'm letting the school deal with him. I've suffered enough."

As if that wasn't chaotic enough, Carl suddenly announced, "Time for my experiment! Everyone grab a helmet!"

"What helmets?" Ellie asked.

Carl disappeared into the hall and came back with a stack of plastic colanders. "We're testing my lice-proof headgear! Pete, grab the glitter cannon!"

"Glitter cannon?!" Claire yelped. "Why do you even have one of those?!"

"Science," Carl said.

We all reluctantly put on colanders while Carl and Pete filled the glitter cannon. Whiskers, sensing more chaos, climbed onto the couch and glared at us like we'd personally offended him.

"Ready, aim... FIRE!" Carl yelled.

Glitter exploded everywhere, and for a moment, it felt like we were in a disco snowstorm. "This is supposed to simulate lice movement!" Carl shouted over the chaos.

"Pretty sure lice don't sparkle," Ellie said, brushing glitter out of her hair.

Claire sneezed. "I'm going to be picking glitter out of my nose for weeks!"

Pete, of course, was loving it. "This is going in the next verse of my rap!" he declared, grabbing the spatula again.

♪ "Glitter lice in the air,
everywhere, beware,
You can't run, you can't hide, but you can prepare!" ♪

At this point, Whiskers had had enough. With a dramatic leap, he knocked over the glitter cannon, sending a final cloud of glitter raining down. Then he sprinted out of the room, probably to plot his revenge.

"Whiskers is going to murder us in our sleep," I muttered.

"Totally worth it," Carl said, grinning as he admired his glittery colander helmet.

Somehow, we managed to clean up enough to start working on posters for Anti-Itch Week. Ellie's hat designs were... let's just say *unique*.

"This one's called 'Lice Are the Real Villains,'" she said, holding up a drawing of a lice monster fighting a superhero with a comb.

"Ellie," I said, "what does that even mean?"

"It's symbolic!" Ellie said.

Claire rolled her eyes. "Yeah, symbolically terrifying."

By the time we finished, the living room looked like a craft store had exploded. Glitter, glue sticks, and mayo-smudged paper were everywhere.

Pete plopped down on the couch, still holding the spatula mic. "You know," he said, "this might've been the best Anti-Itch planning session in history."

"Minus the glitter cannon," Claire said, removing a sparkly speck off her shirt.

"Minus Whiskers plotting his revenge," I added.

"Minus Ellie's pizza hat idea," Claire muttered.

Ellie gasped. "The pizza hat is genius!"

"Let's just agree we all survived," I said, shaking glitter out of my hair. "Barely."

As chaotic as it was, I had to admit—it was nice to have some laughs in the middle of all this lice madness. Even if my living room would never recover.

10. Dancing, Drama, and the Lice Patrol

The Anti-Itch Dance was finally here, and let me tell you, it was the most *chaotic* thing our school had ever pulled off. I'm not saying it was perfect—Ellie's "lice-free fashion booth" ended up with glitter everywhere (again), and Carl tried to sneak in his glitter cannon—but it was exactly the kind of ridiculous fun we all needed.

The cafeteria had been transformed with banners that said stuff like *"Dance Your Itch Off!"* and *"Hats, Not Scratches!"* There was even a giant, glittery lice comb hanging from the ceiling, which Pete called "a bold design choice" while everyone else just called it "gross."

Ellie had outdone herself with her hat. She was wearing what can only be described as a **pizza masterpiece**—a red beret covered in fake pepperonis and sparkly cheese. "It's symbolic," she said proudly.

"Symbolic of what?" Claire asked.

"Of never underestimating the power of creativity!" Ellie replied.

"Symbolic of hunger," Pete muttered, eyeing the fake pepperonis.

Meanwhile, the DJ (a.k.a. Pete's older brother, who owed Pete money) was blasting all kind of music. Kids were on the dance floor, awkwardly shuffling and scratching in time to the beat. It was the first time scratching was officially *encouraged* at a school event.

"Slide to the left... now scratch!"

"Slide to the right... now itch!"

Even the teachers got into it. Mr. Dawson tried to show off some breakdancing moves, and I swear, I saw Nurse Daniels, doing the sprinkler. Except she had a lice comb in one hand, ready to pounce on anyone who scratched *too much*.

Claire nudged me and pointed at the snack table. "Check it out—Pete's getting ready to perform his rap."

Sure enough, Pete was standing on a chair, wearing sunglasses and holding the dreaded spatula mic.

♪ "Yo, DJ Scratch is in the house,
No louse, just sauce,
Put your hats in the air, no need to floss!" ♪

The crowd went wild—or maybe they were just trying to drown him out. Either way, Pete was having the time of his life, and Carl was his unofficial hype man, jumping around in a glitter-covered colander hat.

Ellie rolled her eyes. "I'm pretending I don't know either of them."

Just when I thought things couldn't get more ridiculous, I spotted Mackenzie Harper across the room. She was wearing the most elaborate hat I'd ever seen—a giant pink sunhat with feathers, rhinestones, and what looked like a live flower arrangement glued to the brim.

Claire followed my gaze. "What is that? A hat or a garden?"

"I think it's both," I said.

Mackenzie was doing her usual strut, but something seemed... off. She kept adjusting her hat like her life depended on it, and every few minutes, she'd glance nervously over her shoulder.

Then it happened.

We were halfway through Pete's second (and unfortunately longer) rap when Mackenzie leaned down to pick up something off the floor. Her hat caught on the edge of a table, and before she could grab it, it fell off.

The entire dance seemed to pause in slow motion as she stood there, her face pale, her hair looking noticeably *not perfect*. For a second, I thought she might try to laugh it off, but instead, she let out a panicked scream and bolted for the door.

"What just happened?" Claire asked, blinking.

"I don't know," I said, already moving. "But I'm gonna find out."

Ellie grabbed my arm. "Are you sure about this? It's Mackenzie Harper."

"Yeah, and she's also a person," I said, shrugging her off. "Be right back."

I weaved through the crowd, ignoring Pete's latest attempt at freestyle rap, and followed Mackenzie out of the gym. She turned a corner and disappeared into the bathroom.

As I reached the bathroom door, I could hear muffled sounds from inside—sniffles, maybe, or someone frantically fixing their hair.

I took a deep breath and stepped closer.

"Mackenzie?" I called out, knocking gently on the door.

No answer.

I hesitated, my hand hovering over the handle. Part of me wanted to walk away and let her deal with whatever was going on by herself. But another part of me—the part that had been the butt of her jokes for years—couldn't help but feel like I had to see this through.

And with that, I opened the door.

11. The Lice Confession & Shampoo Shenanigans

The bathroom was so quiet you could hear the music still playing from the gym. I stood there awkwardly, watching Mackenzie Harper crouched by the sinks, her hands buried in her hair.

Her sparkly pink sunhat was stuffed under her arm, and for the first time ever, Mackenzie didn't look perfect. She looked...well, human.

"Do you mind?" she snapped, glaring at me through her fingers.

"Uh, sorry," I said, backing up slightly. "But you kinda ran out of there like the gym was on fire. I just wanted to check—"

"I'm fine!" she interrupted, then groaned and let her head fall against the counter.

I raised an eyebrow. "You sure about that?"

She groaned louder. "Okay, fine. I'm not fine! Are you happy now?"

"Not really," I said, leaning against the door. "What's going on, Mackenzie? And don't say 'nothing,' because you just left your friends to fend off Pete's freestyle rapping."

She snorted laughing, but then her face wrinkled like a raisin. "I have lice, okay?! I'm *patient zero!* Are you happy now?"

I blinked. "Wait, what?"

She waved her hands dramatically. "I'm the reason the whole school is scratching their heads like maniacs! I noticed it last week, but I couldn't tell anyone because, well—look at me!"

I tilted my head. "Uh, you look fine."

"No, I don't!" she hissed. "My hair has been a disaster all week. I've tried *everything*—hats, sprays, glitter glue, everything! But those stupid lice just keep coming back."

I couldn't help it. I laughed.

Mackenzie glared at me. "What's so funny?"

"It's just…" I said, trying to compose myself, "you've been going around calling everyone else 'lice losers,' and you're the one with the lice? That's, like, peak irony."

"Ha-ha, hilarious," she said, rolling her eyes.

"But seriously," I said, sitting down on the floor across from her. "Why haven't you just treated it? There's shampoo for that."

Her face turned bright red. "Do you think I don't know that? But if I go to the store and buy lice shampoo, everyone will *know*! Can you imagine what that would do to my reputation?"

I shrugged. "I mean, probably not worse than being the secret lice queen of the school."

She groaned again. "You don't get it, Avery. I'm Mackenzie Harper. People look up to me."

"Sure, okay," I said, trying not to roll my eyes. "But you're also just…a kid. And kids get lice. It's not the end of the world."

She stared at me for a long moment, then muttered, "Easy for you to say."

I sighed. "Look, I have some lice shampoo at home. You can have it if you want."

Mackenzie's head snapped up. "You do?"

"Yeah," I said. "But you're gonna have to come get it. No way am I bringing it to school."

She hesitated, then nodded. "Fine. But you can't tell *anyone*. Not Ellie, not Claire, not your weird brother—no one."

"Deal," I said, holding out my hand. She looked at it like I'd just offered her a dead fish, but eventually, she shook it.

That evening, things at my house were as chaotic as ever. Carl and Pete were in the living room wearing trash bags over their head. Typical Monday.

"This is how you get rid of lice naturally," Carl announced, balancing a jar of mayo on his head.

Pete added, "And also how you attract every stray cat in the neighborhood."

Whiskers, who was still salty from being part of Carl's "security patrol," sat on the couch glaring at them like he was plotting their demise.

"You guys look ridiculous," I said, walking past with a plate of pizza.

"Ridiculous or genius?" Carl asked, grinning through a glob of mayonnaise.

"Definitely ridiculous," I said, shaking my head.

Just then, there was a knock at the door. I opened it to find Mackenzie Harper standing there in the weirdest disguise I'd ever seen: a giant hoodie, sunglasses, and a baseball cap pulled low over her face. She looked like she was auditioning for *Undercover Celebrity: The Lice Edition*.

"Seriously?" I said, raising an eyebrow.

"Do you want me to get caught?" she hissed, glancing over her shoulder.

"No one cares that much," I said, letting her in.

As soon as Mackenzie stepped inside, Carl and Pete froze.

"Whoa," Pete said, staring at her. "Is that—?"

"Nope," I interrupted. "Not who you think. Just someone here to borrow a book."

Carl squinted at Mackenzie. "Why is your 'friend' wearing sunglasses indoors?"

"She's shy," I said, shoving Mackenzie toward the stairs. "Stay out of it, Carl."

Carl looked skeptical, but thankfully, he didn't follow us. Upstairs, I grabbed the lice shampoo from the bathroom and handed it to Mackenzie.

"Here," I said. "One bottle of miracle cure."

She took it like it was made of gold. "Thanks."

"No problem," I said. "Just, uh, don't forget to actually use it."

She rolled her eyes but nodded. "Yeah, yeah."

As she turned to leave, she paused. "Hey, Avery?"

"Yeah?"

She hesitated. "Thanks. I mean it."

I smiled. "Don't mention it. Really. Don't."

Mackenzie smirked, then slipped out the door like a spy on a top-secret mission. I watched her go, shaking my head.

Who would've thought I'd be smuggling lice shampoo to Mackenzie Harper?

12. Victory, Lice-Free-ish

The school day started like a dream—Principal Walder stood at the podium in the gym during morning announcements, proudly declaring, "The lice outbreak is officially under control!"

The gym erupted into cheers, high-fives, and a few cartwheels. It was the kind of celebration you'd expect if we'd just won a state championship, not beaten tiny, vampire bugs. But hey, we'd take the win.

"Thanks to community effort and mutual support," Principal Walder continued, puffing out his chest like we'd all just survived a natural disaster, "we can now focus on learning and growing lice-free!"

Mackenzie Harper, sitting a few rows ahead of me, let out a very audible sigh and whispered something to her friends. They all rolled their eyes in perfect synchronized Queen Bee fashion.

But then—this part nearly made me spit out my gum—Mackenzie turned around, locked eyes with me, and gave me a tiny, reluctant nod. Not a wave, not a smile. Just a nod.

Claire gasped next to me. "Did Mackenzie Harper just acknowledge your existence?"

"I think so," I whispered back, blinking in disbelief.

"Does this mean you're cool now?" Ellie asked, grinning.

I shrugged. "Let's not get ahead of ourselves, folks"

At lunch, the cafeteria was buzzing with a "lice-free energy." People were finally sharing hats again, which I thought was wildly optimistic considering how recently we'd all been scratching.

I was halfway through my peanut butter sandwich when Jason—the Jason, who was one grade ahead of me and approximately the most perfect human being alive—walked up to my table.

"Hey, Avery," he said casually, like he hadn't just turned my insides into jelly.

I froze mid-bite, the sandwich sticking to the roof of my mouth. Ellie kicked me under the table, and I managed to swallow.

"H-Hi, Jason," I stammered.

"I just wanted to say..." He paused, running a hand through his perfect hair. "That dance you and your friends put together? It was really cool. You're cool."

I almost dropped my sandwich. Ellie looked like she was about to burst into song, and Claire was mouthing, *Say something!*

"Uh, thanks!" I finally managed, my face approximately the color of ketchup. "I'm glad you liked it."

Jason smiled—*smiled!*—and I was about to say something brilliant, like maybe suggest we do a group project sometime, when—

"AVERY!"

I turned to see Nurse Daniels, marching toward me with her lice comb in hand. My heart sank.

"Uh...hi, Nurse Daniels," I said, already dreading what was coming.

"I need you for a recheck," she said, her tone leaving no room for argument.

"A recheck?" I repeated, my stomach sinking.

"Yes," she said firmly. "Right now."

And just like that, my brief moment of glory came crashing down.

"Sure," I said weakly, standing up while Claire and Ellie tried (and failed) to hide their laughter.

As I followed Nurse Daniels out of the cafeteria, I couldn't help but think that surviving middle school wasn't just about beating lice. It was about surviving *everything*—from embarrassing moments to Queen Bees, to comb-wielding nurses.

And clearly, my battle wasn't over yet.

"Avery," Nurse Daniels said as she opened the nurse's office door. "This time, I'm checking *twice*."

Printed in Dunstable, United Kingdom

64992319R00030